OUR
BUCKET LIST
ADVENTURES

- A Journal for Couples -

ASHLEY AND MARCUS KUSI

Our Bucket List Adventures: A Journal for Couples

Created by Ashley and Marcus Kusi.

ISBN-13: 978-0-9987291-7-6

ISBN-10: 0-9987291-7-5

Getting Started

"Twenty years from now you will be more disappointed by the things you didn't do than by the ones you did do. So throw off the bowlines. Sail away from the safe harbor. Catch the trade winds in your sails. Explore. Dream. Discover."

– H. Jackson Brown Jr.'s mother

The unique experiences we share with those we love are the memories we remember the most. From our experience, accomplishing a bucket list goal together is a priceless experience. It's also a great way to strengthen intimacy and grow together as a couple.

That's why we created *Our Bucket List Adventures*, a bucket list journal to make it easier for you and your partner to sit down, dream together, and create 50 exciting bucket list goals you want to experience together. After making your dreams a reality, it will also be the place to journal your bucket list memories and add a photo or scrapbook memorabilia.

Our Bucket List Adventures is designed to encourage couples like you to get out there and adventure together. It has 50 journal entries to guide you in planning, recording, and reflecting on the top 50 bucket list adventures you want to experience together.

First, you will find 115 bucket list ideas to help you get started. We've also included an activity list of categories for you and your partner to fill in with what you both truly want to experience together. This activity will help you narrow down your bucket list ideas.

Second, you will find an index table for organizing your completed bucket list items, so that you can easily find where you journaled it, because accomplishing your goals may not follow a linear path.

Third, comes the journal itself. There is space at the top to write down which bucket list item you chose, with space below to record the date you accomplished this dream and to write down fun memories from the experience.

Lastly, opposite each journaling page is space for you to paste a photo or two to help you reminisce the adventure you shared together, plus five activity questions (conversation starters) to guide your reflections so you get the most out of your experience.

Now, choose your top 50 bucket list ideas together, write them down, and start planning your adventures!

"The purpose of life, after all, is to live it, to taste experience to the utmost, to reach out eagerly and without fear for newer and richer experience."

– Eleanor Roosevelt

115 Bucket List Ideas for Couples

With your partner, circle or highlight the ideas to use in your bucket list

1. Swim with dolphins or sharks
2. Throw a dart at a map and go wherever it lands
3. Ride in a hot air balloon
4. Add a lock to the love lock bridge in Paris
5. Go ocean fishing
6. Ride a horse on the beach
7. Buy a home
8. Go skydiving
9. Visit all the continents in the world
10. Stay in an overwater bungalow
11. Adopt a shelter pet
12. See the eight world wonders: Pyramids at Giza, Temple of Artemis at Ephesus, Hanging Gardens of Babylon, Lighthouse of Alexandria, Statue of Zeus at Olympia, Mausoleum at Halicarnassus, Colossus of Rhodes, and Stonehenge in England
13. Rent a beach house for the whole summer

14. Rent a glass igloo in Finland to sleep under the northern lights

15. Dine in an underwater restaurant

16. Go to Disneyland

17. Go scuba diving

18. Take a road trip

19. Watch a meteor shower or eclipse

20. Buy a homeless person a full meal, clean clothes, shower, haircut and a night off the street

21. Go to a drive-in movie

22. See a live event in a stadium: sports, stand-up comedy, music concert, etc.

23. Play paintball

24. Fly a plane

25. Travel to a place or country you have never been together

26. Go whale watching

27. Say "yes" to everything for a day

28. Go to the Olympics, World Cup, or another international event

29. Go parasailing

30. Pay for a stranger's groceries or dinner at a restaurant

31. Make food and pass it out to the homeless

32. Adopt a child

33. Learn a new language

34. See a Broadway play

35. Ride in a private jet

36. Design your own house and build it

37. Go to a masquerade ball

38. Visit every major landmark in your country or state

39. Complete an obstacle race: Spartan, Tough Mudder, Zombie Mud Run, etc.

40. Write a book

41. Float in the Dead Sea

42. Have a baby

43. Spend New Year's in Times Square

44. Go sailing

45. Visit the Haiku Stairs in Oahu, Hawaii

46. Explore or spend a night in a real castle

47. Attend a class or workshop: cooking, art, glass blowing, pottery, chocolate making, brewery, etc.

48. Make a wish at the Trevi Fountain in Rome

49. Dive in a submarine and see the Titanic

50. Visit a glow worm cave

51. Visit Machu Picchu, Peru

52. See the Hobbit town in New Zealand

53. Go dogsledding

54. Go white water rafting

55. Complete a 5/5 star geocache

56. Hike the Grand Canyon

57. Spend the night at the ice hotel in Quebec

58. Spend Christmas in Aspen

59. Experience 24 hours of daylight in Alaska

60. Climb a glacier

61. Swim in the Great Barrier Reef

62. Hike the 54 fourteeners in Colorado

63. Swim in every ocean

64. Experience weightlessness

65. Hug a redwood

66. Go skinny-dipping together

67. Try chocolate-covered ants

68. Drink at a distillery

69. Eat a meal cooked by a celebrity chef

70. Eat a molecular gastronomy dinner

71. Learn a new instrument

72. Sing in public together

73. Learn ballroom or salsa dancing together

74. Name a star

75. Sponsor a child

76. Attend a film premiere

77. Get VIP passes to a show/concert

78. Become financially independent

79. Start a side business

80. Give money in an envelope anonymously to a stranger, or even someone you know

81. See Cirque du Soleil

82. Get tattoos together

83. Go backpacking through Europe

84. Try role-playing

85. Use a new sex toy

86. Have sex somewhere new

87. Carve our initials into a tree

88. Go camping together

89. Go paddleboarding

90. Spend a day at a spa and have a couple's massage

91. Live in a different country

92. Get married

93. Gamble in Vegas

94. Go snorkeling

95. Run a 5k together

96. Visit an ancient city

97. Participate in an archaeological dig

98. Go on a safari in Africa

99. Go to a museum together

100. Ride camels across a desert

101. Attend a wine tasting

102. Have a couple's book club; read the same books and then discuss

103. Charter a yacht

104. Host a couple's game night or family game night

105. Have sex outside

106. Try a winter sport: skiing, snowmobiling, snowboarding, skating, etc.

107. Dance on the beach at sunset

108. RV across a country

109. Volunteer together

110. Go to a conference or convention together about relationships or other topics that are important to both of you

111. Give a speech together

112. Plan a surprise trip for each other, whether birthday or spontaneous

113. Go rock climbing together

114. Orgasm at the same time

115. Build an orphanage or school

Bucket List Activities

Take turns filling in the blanks for each category

Places

Travel in country:

_____

_____

_____

_____

Travel outside of the country:

_____

_____

_____

_____

Beaches, natural/mineral springs, lakes:

_____

_____

_____

_____

Places that are fun, mysterious, relaxing, etc.:

_____

_____

_____

_____

Foods or Restaurants to Try

_____

_____

_____

_____

Food, beer or gastro type festivals to attend:

_____

_____

_____

_____

Activities to Do Together

Mountains to climb, trails to hike, rivers to canoe or kayak. Train for a race or competition, drive a dream car, mountain bike, go fishing, whale watch, etc.

_____

_____

_____

_____

_____

_____

Free or Inexpensive Things

Such as: community, sports and active activities.

_____

_____

_____

_____

_____

Volunteering, helping, giving, teaching, or protesting:

_____

_____

_____

_____

_____

Goals as A Couple

Such as family, career, finances, sex and intimacy, etc.

_____

_____

_____

Have sex in/on/while:

_____

_____

_____

Buy:

_____

_____

_____

Attend a:

_____

_____

_____

Things to experience – weird, uncomfortable, challenging, and exciting adventures you have always wanted to do that are out of your comfort zone:

_____

_____

_____

_____

_____

Personal Growth

Take a class/course on:

_____

_____

_____

_____

Make, create, write:

_____

_____

_____

_____

Quit or give up:

_____

_____

_____

_____

Develop more:

_____

_____

_____

_____

Fun

Sports to play or attend events:

_____

_____

_____

_____

Things/places to see/do/go:

_____

_____

_____

_____

Seasonal

Spring:

_____

_____

_____

Summer:

_____

_____

_____

Fall:

_____

_____

_____

Winter:

_____

_____

_____

Three Things You Want to Do Together Before You Die

_____

_____

_____

_____

_____

Bucket List Goal Finder

Bucket List Goal	Page #	Bucket List Goal	Page #

Bucket List Goal Finder

Bucket List Goal	Page #	Bucket List Goal	Page #

Bucket List Item _____

Date Accomplished _____

Our Memories

_____

_____

_____

_____

_____

_____

_____

_____

_____

_____

_____

_____

_____

Discuss

- What was your favorite part?
- What was your least favorite part?
- What did you learn about yourself? Your partner?
- What would you do different next time?
- What bucket list item are you looking forward to next?

Our Favorite Photos

Bucket List Item _____

Date Accomplished _____

Our Memories

_____
_____
_____
_____
_____
_____
_____
_____
_____
_____
_____
_____
_____
_____

Discuss

- What was your favorite part?
- What was your least favorite part?
- What did you learn about yourself? Your partner?
- What would you do different next time?
- What bucket list item are you looking forward to next?

Our Favorite Photos

3

Bucket List Item _____

Date Accomplished _____

Our Memories

_____

_____

_____

_____

_____

_____

_____

_____

_____

_____

_____

_____

_____

_____

Discuss

- What was your favorite part?
- What was your least favorite part?
- What did you learn about yourself? Your partner?
- What would you do different next time?
- What bucket list item are you looking forward to next?

Our Favorite Photos

4

Bucket List Item _____

Date Accomplished _____

Our Memories

_____
_____
_____
_____
_____
_____
_____
_____
_____
_____
_____
_____
_____
_____

Discuss

- What was your favorite part?
- What was your least favorite part?
- What did you learn about yourself? Your partner?
- What would you do different next time?
- What bucket list item are you looking forward to next?

Our Favorite Photos

5

Bucket List Item _____

Date Accomplished _____

Our Memories

_____

_____

_____

_____

_____

_____

_____

_____

_____

_____

_____

_____

_____

Discuss

- What was your favorite part?
- What was your least favorite part?
- What did you learn about yourself? Your partner?
- What would you do different next time?
- What bucket list item are you looking forward to next?

Our Favorite Photos

Bucket List Item _____

Date Accomplished _____

Our Memories

_____
_____
_____
_____
_____
_____
_____
_____
_____
_____
_____
_____
_____
_____
_____
_____

Discuss

- What was your favorite part?
- What was your least favorite part?
- What did you learn about yourself? Your partner?
- What would you do different next time?
- What bucket list item are you looking forward to next?

Our Favorite Photos

Bucket List Item _____

Date Accomplished _____

Our Memories

_____
_____
_____
_____
_____
_____
_____
_____
_____
_____
_____
_____
_____

Discuss

- What was your favorite part?
- What was your least favorite part?
- What did you learn about yourself? Your partner?
- What would you do different next time?
- What bucket list item are you looking forward to next?

Our Favorite Photos

Bucket List Item _____

Date Accomplished _____

Our Memories

_____

_____

_____

_____

_____

_____

_____

_____

_____

_____

_____

_____

_____

Discuss

- What was your favorite part?
- What was your least favorite part?
- What did you learn about yourself? Your partner?
- What would you do different next time?
- What bucket list item are you looking forward to next?

Our Favorite Photos

9

Bucket List Item _____

Date Accomplished _____

Our Memories

_____

_____

_____

_____

_____

_____

_____

_____

_____

_____

_____

_____

_____

Discuss

- What was your favorite part?
- What was your least favorite part?
- What did you learn about yourself? Your partner?
- What would you do different next time?
- What bucket list item are you looking forward to next?

Our Favorite Photos

10

Bucket List Item _____

Date Accomplished _____

Our Memories

_____
_____
_____
_____
_____
_____
_____
_____
_____
_____
_____
_____
_____
_____

Discuss

- What was your favorite part?
- What was your least favorite part?
- What did you learn about yourself? Your partner?
- What would you do different next time?
- What bucket list item are you looking forward to next?

Our Favorite Photos

Bucket List Item _____

Date Accomplished _____

Our Memories

_____

_____

_____

_____

_____

_____

_____

_____

_____

_____

_____

_____

_____

Discuss

- What was your favorite part?
- What was your least favorite part?
- What did you learn about yourself? Your partner?
- What would you do different next time?
- What bucket list item are you looking forward to next?

Our Favorite Photos

12

Bucket List Item _____

Date Accomplished _____

Our Memories

_____

_____

_____

_____

_____

_____

_____

_____

_____

_____

_____

_____

_____

_____

_____

Discuss

- What was your favorite part?
- What was your least favorite part?
- What did you learn about yourself? Your partner?
- What would you do different next time?
- What bucket list item are you looking forward to next?

Our Favorite Photos

13

Bucket List Item _____

Date Accomplished _____

Our Memories

_____
_____
_____
_____
_____
_____
_____
_____
_____
_____
_____
_____
_____
_____

Discuss

- What was your favorite part?
- What was your least favorite part?
- What did you learn about yourself? Your partner?
- What would you do different next time?
- What bucket list item are you looking forward to next?

Our Favorite Photos

14

Bucket List Item _____

Date Accomplished _____

Our Memories

_____
_____
_____
_____
_____
_____
_____
_____
_____
_____
_____
_____
_____
_____

Discuss

- What was your favorite part?
- What was your least favorite part?
- What did you learn about yourself? Your partner?
- What would you do different next time?
- What bucket list item are you looking forward to next?

Our Favorite Photos

15 Bucket List Item _____

Date Accomplished _____

Our Memories

_____
_____
_____
_____
_____
_____
_____
_____
_____
_____
_____
_____
_____
_____

Discuss

- What was your favorite part?
- What was your least favorite part?
- What did you learn about yourself? Your partner?
- What would you do different next time?
- What bucket list item are you looking forward to next?

Our Favorite Photos

16

Bucket List Item _____

Date Accomplished _____

Our Memories

_____
_____
_____
_____
_____
_____
_____
_____
_____
_____
_____
_____
_____
_____

Discuss

- What was your favorite part?
- What was your least favorite part?
- What did you learn about yourself? Your partner?
- What would you do different next time?
- What bucket list item are you looking forward to next?

Our Favorite Photos

17

Bucket List Item _____

Date Accomplished _____

Our Memories

_____
_____
_____
_____
_____
_____
_____
_____
_____
_____
_____
_____
_____
_____

Discuss

- What was your favorite part?
- What was your least favorite part?
- What did you learn about yourself? Your partner?
- What would you do different next time?
- What bucket list item are you looking forward to next?

Our Favorite Photos

Bucket List Item _____

Date Accomplished _____

Our Memories

_____
_____
_____
_____
_____
_____
_____
_____
_____
_____
_____
_____
_____

Discuss

- What was your favorite part?
- What was your least favorite part?
- What did you learn about yourself? Your partner?
- What would you do different next time?
- What bucket list item are you looking forward to next?

Our Favorite Photos

19

Bucket List Item _____

Date Accomplished _____

Our Memories

_____
_____
_____
_____
_____
_____
_____
_____
_____
_____
_____
_____
_____
_____

Discuss

- What was your favorite part?
- What was your least favorite part?
- What did you learn about yourself? Your partner?
- What would you do different next time?
- What bucket list item are you looking forward to next?

Our Favorite Photos

20

Bucket List Item _____

Date Accomplished _____

Our Memories

_____

_____

_____

_____

_____

_____

_____

_____

_____

_____

_____

_____

_____

_____

Discuss

- What was your favorite part?
- What was your least favorite part?
- What did you learn about yourself? Your partner?
- What would you do different next time?
- What bucket list item are you looking forward to next?

Our Favorite Photos

Bucket List Item _____

Date Accomplished _____

Our Memories

_____
_____
_____
_____
_____
_____
_____
_____
_____
_____
_____
_____
_____

Discuss

- What was your favorite part?
- What was your least favorite part?
- What did you learn about yourself? Your partner?
- What would you do different next time?
- What bucket list item are you looking forward to next?

Our Favorite Photos

22

Bucket List Item _____

Date Accomplished _____

Our Memories

_____

_____

_____

_____

_____

_____

_____

_____

_____

_____

_____

_____

_____

_____

Discuss

- What was your favorite part?
- What was your least favorite part?
- What did you learn about yourself? Your partner?
- What would you do different next time?
- What bucket list item are you looking forward to next?

Our Favorite Photos

23

Bucket List Item _____

Date Accomplished _____

Our Memories

_____
_____
_____
_____
_____
_____
_____
_____
_____
_____
_____
_____
_____
_____

Discuss

- What was your favorite part?
- What was your least favorite part?
- What did you learn about yourself? Your partner?
- What would you do different next time?
- What bucket list item are you looking forward to next?

Our Favorite Photos

24 Bucket List Item _____

Date Accomplished _____

Our Memories

_____
_____
_____
_____
_____
_____
_____
_____
_____
_____
_____
_____
_____

Discuss

- What was your favorite part?
- What was your least favorite part?
- What did you learn about yourself? Your partner?
- What would you do different next time?
- What bucket list item are you looking forward to next?

Our Favorite Photos

25

Bucket List Item _____

Date Accomplished _____

Our Memories

_____
_____
_____
_____
_____
_____
_____
_____
_____
_____
_____
_____
_____
_____
_____

Discuss

- What was your favorite part?
- What was your least favorite part?
- What did you learn about yourself? Your partner?
- What would you do different next time?
- What bucket list item are you looking forward to next?

Our Favorite Photos

26

Bucket List Item _____

Date Accomplished _____

Our Memories

_____
_____
_____
_____
_____
_____
_____
_____
_____
_____
_____
_____
_____
_____

Discuss

- What was your favorite part?
- What was your least favorite part?
- What did you learn about yourself? Your partner?
- What would you do different next time?
- What bucket list item are you looking forward to next?

Our Favorite Photos

27

Bucket List Item _____

Date Accomplished _____

Our Memories

_____
_____
_____
_____
_____
_____
_____
_____
_____
_____
_____
_____
_____
_____
_____

Discuss

- What was your favorite part?
- What was your least favorite part?
- What did you learn about yourself? Your partner?
- What would you do different next time?
- What bucket list item are you looking forward to next?

Our Favorite Photos

Bucket List Item _____

Date Accomplished _____

Our Memories

_____

_____

_____

_____

_____

_____

_____

_____

_____

_____

_____

_____

_____

_____

Discuss

- What was your favorite part?
- What was your least favorite part?
- What did you learn about yourself? Your partner?
- What would you do different next time?
- What bucket list item are you looking forward to next?

Our Favorite Photos

29

Bucket List Item _____

Date Accomplished _____

Our Memories

_____
_____
_____
_____
_____
_____
_____
_____
_____
_____
_____
_____
_____

Discuss

- What was your favorite part?
- What was your least favorite part?
- What did you learn about yourself? Your partner?
- What would you do different next time?
- What bucket list item are you looking forward to next?

Our Favorite Photos

30

Bucket List Item _____

Date Accomplished _____

Our Memories

_____
_____
_____
_____
_____
_____
_____
_____
_____
_____
_____
_____
_____

Discuss

- What was your favorite part?
- What was your least favorite part?
- What did you learn about yourself? Your partner?
- What would you do different next time?
- What bucket list item are you looking forward to next?

Our Favorite Photos

31

Bucket List Item _____

Date Accomplished _____

Our Memories

_____
_____
_____
_____
_____
_____
_____
_____
_____
_____
_____
_____
_____
_____

Discuss

- What was your favorite part?
- What was your least favorite part?
- What did you learn about yourself? Your partner?
- What would you do different next time?
- What bucket list item are you looking forward to next?

Our Favorite Photos

32

Bucket List Item _____

Date Accomplished _____

Our Memories

_____

_____

_____

_____

_____

_____

_____

_____

_____

_____

_____

_____

_____

_____

Discuss

- What was your favorite part?
- What was your least favorite part?
- What did you learn about yourself? Your partner?
- What would you do different next time?
- What bucket list item are you looking forward to next?

Our Favorite Photos

33

Bucket List Item _____

Date Accomplished _____

Our Memories

_____
_____
_____
_____
_____
_____
_____
_____
_____
_____
_____
_____
_____

Discuss

- What was your favorite part?
- What was your least favorite part?
- What did you learn about yourself? Your partner?
- What would you do different next time?
- What bucket list item are you looking forward to next?

Our Favorite Photos

34

Bucket List Item _____

Date Accomplished _____

Our Memories

_____
_____
_____
_____
_____
_____
_____
_____
_____
_____
_____
_____
_____
_____

Discuss

- What was your favorite part?
- What was your least favorite part?
- What did you learn about yourself? Your partner?
- What would you do different next time?
- What bucket list item are you looking forward to next?

Our Favorite Photos

35

Bucket List Item _____

Our Memories

_____
_____
_____
_____
_____
_____
_____
_____
_____
_____
_____
_____
_____
_____

Discuss

- What was your favorite part?
- What was your least favorite part?
- What did you learn about yourself? Your partner?
- What would you do different next time?
- What bucket list item are you looking forward to next?

Our Favorite Photos

36

Bucket List Item _____

Date Accomplished _____

Our Memories

_____
_____
_____
_____
_____
_____
_____
_____
_____
_____
_____
_____
_____
_____

Discuss

- What was your favorite part?
- What was your least favorite part?
- What did you learn about yourself? Your partner?
- What would you do different next time?
- What bucket list item are you looking forward to next?

Our Favorite Photos

37

Bucket List Item _____

Date Accomplished _____

Our Memories

_____

_____

_____

_____

_____

_____

_____

_____

_____

_____

_____

_____

Discuss

- What was your favorite part?
- What was your least favorite part?
- What did you learn about yourself? Your partner?
- What would you do different next time?
- What bucket list item are you looking forward to next?

Our Favorite Photos

38

Bucket List Item _____

Date Accomplished _____

Our Memories

_____

_____

_____

_____

_____

_____

_____

_____

_____

_____

_____

_____

_____

Discuss

- What was your favorite part?
- What was your least favorite part?
- What did you learn about yourself? Your partner?
- What would you do different next time?
- What bucket list item are you looking forward to next?

Our Favorite Photos

39

Bucket List Item _____

Date Accomplished _____

Our Memories

_____
_____
_____
_____
_____
_____
_____
_____
_____
_____
_____
_____
_____
_____

Discuss

- What was your favorite part?
- What was your least favorite part?
- What did you learn about yourself? Your partner?
- What would you do different next time?
- What bucket list item are you looking forward to next?

Our Favorite Photos

40

Bucket List Item _____

Date Accomplished _____

Our Memories

_____
_____
_____
_____
_____
_____
_____
_____
_____
_____
_____
_____
_____
_____

Discuss

- What was your favorite part?
- What was your least favorite part?
- What did you learn about yourself? Your partner?
- What would you do different next time?
- What bucket list item are you looking forward to next?

Our Favorite Photos

41

Bucket List Item _____

Date Accomplished _____

Our Memories

_____
_____
_____
_____
_____
_____
_____
_____
_____
_____
_____
_____
_____
_____

Discuss

- What was your favorite part?
- What was your least favorite part?
- What did you learn about yourself? Your partner?
- What would you do different next time?
- What bucket list item are you looking forward to next?

Our Favorite Photos

42

Bucket List Item _____

Date Accomplished _____

Our Memories

_____
_____
_____
_____
_____
_____
_____
_____
_____
_____
_____
_____
_____
_____
_____
_____

Discuss

- What was your favorite part?
- What was your least favorite part?
- What did you learn about yourself? Your partner?
- What would you do different next time?
- What bucket list item are you looking forward to next?

Our Favorite Photos

43

Bucket List Item _____

Date Accomplished _____

Our Memories

_____
_____
_____
_____
_____
_____
_____
_____
_____
_____
_____
_____
_____

Discuss

- What was your favorite part?
- What was your least favorite part?
- What did you learn about yourself? Your partner?
- What would you do different next time?
- What bucket list item are you looking forward to next?

Our Favorite Photos

Bucket List Item _____

Date Accomplished _____

Our Memories

_____
_____
_____
_____
_____
_____
_____
_____
_____
_____
_____
_____
_____
_____

Discuss

- What was your favorite part?
- What was your least favorite part?
- What did you learn about yourself? Your partner?
- What would you do different next time?
- What bucket list item are you looking forward to next?

Our Favorite Photos

45

Bucket List Item _____

Date Accomplished _____

Our Memories

_____
_____
_____
_____
_____
_____
_____
_____
_____
_____
_____
_____
_____

Discuss

- What was your favorite part?
- What was your least favorite part?
- What did you learn about yourself? Your partner?
- What would you do different next time?
- What bucket list item are you looking forward to next?

Our Favorite Photos

46

Bucket List Item _____

Date Accomplished _____

Our Memories

_____
_____
_____
_____
_____
_____
_____
_____
_____
_____
_____
_____
_____
_____
_____

Discuss

- What was your favorite part?
- What was your least favorite part?
- What did you learn about yourself? Your partner?
- What would you do different next time?
- What bucket list item are you looking forward to next?

Our Favorite Photos

47

Bucket List Item _____

Date Accomplished _____

Our Memories

_____
_____
_____
_____
_____
_____
_____
_____
_____
_____
_____
_____
_____
_____

Discuss

- What was your favorite part?
- What was your least favorite part?
- What did you learn about yourself? Your partner?
- What would you do different next time?
- What bucket list item are you looking forward to next?

Our Favorite Photos

48

Bucket List Item _____

Date Accomplished _____

Our Memories

_____
_____
_____
_____
_____
_____
_____
_____
_____
_____
_____
_____
_____
_____
_____
_____

Discuss

- What was your favorite part?
- What was your least favorite part?
- What did you learn about yourself? Your partner?
- What would you do different next time?
- What bucket list item are you looking forward to next?

Our Favorite Photos

Bucket List Item _____

Date Accomplished _____

Our Memories

_____

_____

_____

_____

_____

_____

_____

_____

_____

_____

_____

_____

_____

_____

_____

Discuss

- What was your favorite part?
- What was your least favorite part?
- What did you learn about yourself? Your partner?
- What would you do different next time?
- What bucket list item are you looking forward to next?

Our Favorite Photos

50

Bucket List Item _____

Date Accomplished _____

Our Memories

_____
_____
_____
_____
_____
_____
_____
_____
_____
_____
_____
_____
_____
_____
_____

Discuss

- What was your favorite part?
- What was your least favorite part?
- What did you learn about yourself? Your partner?
- What would you do different next time?
- What bucket list item are you looking forward to next?

Our Favorite Photos

Thank you

Thank you for choosing our bucket list journal! We are very thankful and excited to help you get the most out of your bucket list adventure experiences with your partner.

If you enjoyed using this book, please leave us a review on Amazon and share the book with other couples. You can even gift this book, as a wedding or anniversary gift, to your friends and family.

If you would like to receive email updates about future books, courses, and more, visit our website today to join our book fan community:

www.ourpeacefulfamily.com/bookfan

Thank you again for choosing our journal!

Marcus & Ashley Kusi

Other Books by Ashley and Marcus

1. **Questions for Couples:** 469 Thought-Provoking Conversation Starters for Connecting, Building Trust, and Rekindling Intimacy

2. **Communication in Marriage:** How to Communicate with Your Spouse Without Fighting

3. **First Year of Marriage:** The Newlywed's Guide to Building a Strong Foundation and Adjusting to Married Life.

4. **Emotional and Sexual Intimacy in Marriage:** How to Connect or Reconnect with Your Spouse, Grow Together, and Strengthen Your Marriage

5. **Mama Bear Kusi's Blank Recipe Book:** A Journal with Templates to Write and Organize All Your Favorite Recipes.

6. **Mama Bear Kusi's Weekly Meal Planner:** A 52-Week Menu Planner with Grocery List for Planning Your Meals.

7. **My Tandem Nursing Journey:** Breastfeeding Through Pregnancy, Labor, Nursing Aversion and Beyond.

About the Authors

Marcus and Ashley help overwhelmed newlyweds adjust to married life, and inspire married couples to improve their marriage so they can become better husbands and wives.

They do this by using their own marriage experience, gleaning wisdom from other married couples, and sharing what works for them through their website and marriage podcast, *The First Year Marriage Show*.

Visit the following website to listen to their podcast.

www.firstyearmarriage.com

To learn more about them, visit www.ourpeacefulfamily.com

Marriage is a lifelong journey that thrives on love, commitment, trust, respect, communication, patience, and companionship.

–Marcus & Ashley Kusi

Made in the USA
San Bernardino, CA
08 September 2019